STOP ME IF YOU'VE HEARD THIS

"Stop me if you've heard this . . ."

STOP ME

IF YOU'VE HEARD THIS

{ *A History and Philosophy of Jokes* }

JIM HOLT

W. W. NORTON & COMPANY

NEW YORK   LONDON

"To a Comedian" reprinted with kind
permission of Richard Wilbur.

For information about permission to reproduce selections from
this book, write to Permissions, W. W. Norton & Company, Inc.,
500 Fifth Avenue, New York, NY 10110

For information about special discounts for bulk purchases, please
contact W. W. Norton Special Sales at specialsales@wwnorton.
com or 800-233-4830

Manufacturing by Courier Westford
Book design by Lovedog Studio
Production manager: Anna Oler

Library of Congress Cataloging-in-Publication Data

Holt, Jim, 1954–
Stop me if you've heard this : a history and philosophy of jokes /
Jim Holt.
p. cm.
Includes bibliographical references and index.
ISBN 978-0-393-34399-1
1. Wit and humor—History and criticism. I. Title.
PN6147.H584 2008
809.7—dc22   2008013202

W. W. Norton & Company, Inc.
500 Fifth Avenue, New York, N.Y. 10110
www.wwnorton.com

W. W. Norton & Company Ltd.
Castle House, 75/76 Wells Street, London W1T 3QT

1 2 3 4 5 6 7 8 9 0

For Inigo Thomas, master of piffle
and sometimes staunch friend

*Haec enim ridentur vel sola vel maxime
quae notant et designant turpitudinem
aliquam non turpiter.*

An indecency decently put is the thing
we laugh at hardest.

—Cicero

CONTENTS

PREFACE

Some years ago I was asked by *The New Yorker* to write a history of jokes and joke collectors for a special humor issue of the magazine. I gladly accepted the assignment, expecting, in the fine tradition of pseudo-scholarly journalism, to crib the piece from an existing history of jokes, which I was sure I could find in the bowels of some research library or other. To my horror I discovered that there was no such work extant; the scholarly community had inexplicably neglected this important area of culture. Therefore I was obliged to write the history of jokes myself. I managed to bring off this irksome task, which was a bit like composing a PhD thesis on the fly, and the article—which furnished the impetus for the present book—appeared in *The New Yorker* as scheduled. In the process I amassed a great number of literary, psychological, and philosophical reflections about jokes, as well as many dubious specimens of the genre. (So repugnant and distasteful are some of them that one might legitimately question whether they should be printed; I have included them only for their clinical/anthropological interest, with no expectation—let alone intention—that they should prove amusing.) Here, then, is the sum of my labors. Some readers will consider it exiguous, but to me it is much of a muchness, and that is more than enough.

ACKNOWLEDGMENTS

I SHOULD LIKE TO THANK Susan Davis, Larissa MacFarquhar, Tim Farrington, Leo Carey, Henry Finder, Robert Silvers (who was kind enough to read much of the manuscript despite his abhorrence of the material), Jared Hohlt, Christopher Turner, Richard Wilbur, Chris Calhoun, Jimmy O'Higgins, Bob Weil, Hélène Dantoine, Christopher Hitchens, Lucas Wittmann, Carol Blue, Jon McMillan, and Leon Wieseltier, all of whom, in one way or another, helped. And I am indebted to Ted Cohen for the cabdriver and eretz-gimmel jokes.

STOP ME IF YOU'VE HEARD THIS

Part I

HISTORY

A FEW YEARS AGO, BROWSING IN A DUSTY used-book store in Maine, I came across a curious volume. It was a fat, tattered paperback bearing the title *Rationale of the Dirty Joke*. Its author, I saw from the sixties-style futuristic cover, was G. Legman. Taking it off the shelf and riffling though its badly oxidized pages, I found that it contained what looked like thousands of erotic and scatological jokes, arranged under such themes as "coital postures," "the big inch," and "zoöphily." These jokes were accompanied by Freudian-style commentary, along with random

animadversions on aspects of sixties life, like zip
codes, hippies, women who swear, and Marshall
McLuhan. The most striking aspect of the volume was the author's esoteric scholarship, exem-
plified by this sentence from the introduction:

Particular attention should be drawn to
three rare works presenting Modern Greek,
Arabic, and other Levantine erotic tales
and foolstories: *La Fleur Lascive Orientale*
("Oxford" [Bruxelles: Gay & Mlle. Doucé],
1882), anonymously translated from the
originals by J.-A. Decourdemanche, an even
rarer English retranslation also existing
("Athens" [Sheffield: Leonard Smithers],
1893); *Contes Licencieux de Constantinople et
de l'Asie Mineure*, collected before 1893 by
Prof. Jean Nicolaidès, and published after his
sudden and mysterious death as the opening
volume of a series imitating *Kryptádia*: "*Con-
tributions au Folklore Erotique*" (Kleinbronn

& Paris: G. Ficker [!], 1906–09, 4 vols.); and especially two modern French chapbooks, one entitled *Histoires Arabes* (Paris: A. Quignon, 1927), ascribed to an admittedly pseudonymous "Khati Cheghlou," and its sequel or supplement, *Les Meilleures Histoires Coloniales* (about 1935).

Noting the fanciful names (G. Ficker, Khati Cheghlou) and the cranky, erudite tone, I began to wonder whether this wasn't a wild Nabokovian put-on. No doubt "G. Legman" itself was a pseudonym; both the initial (G-spot?) and the surname (as opposed to tit-man?) were suspicious. But a few months later, in the late winter of 1999, I saw on the obituary page of the *New York Times* that Gershon Legman, a "self-taught scholar of dirty jokes," had died, at the age of eighty-one, in the South of France, where he lived in voluntary exile from his native United States.

A certain facetiousness might seem to attach

to the phrase "scholar of dirty jokes." Is this really an area in which scholarship is appropriate or profitable? Well, jokes do fall into the category of folklore, along with myths, proverbs, legends, nursery rhymes, riddles, and superstitions. And a good proportion of the jokes in oral circulation involve sex or scatology. (An analysis of 13,804 jokes current in New York in 1963 revealed that 17 percent of them were about sex and 11 percent were about "Negroes.") If the history of folklore aspires to be a history of the human mind, as some of its practitioners insist, somebody has to do the tedious job of collecting and recording obscene, disgusting, and blasphemous jokes, and ushering them into print.

Although we think of the joke as a cultural constant, it is a form of humor that comes and goes with the rise and fall of civilizations. What distinguishes the joke from the mere humorous tale is that it climaxes in a punch line—a little verbal explosion set off by a sudden switch in meaning.

6

A joke, unlike a tale, wants to be brief. As Freud observed, it says what it has to say not just in few words but in *too* few words. There is, of course, a longer genre of joke known as the "shaggy-dog story" in which digressions and embroideries lead to an almost painfully delayed punch line. But the classic joke proceeds with arrowlike swiftness, resolving its matter in the form of a two-liner (*Hear about the bulimic stag party? The cake came out of the girl*) or even a one-liner (*I was so ugly when I was born, the doctor slapped my mother*). Often it is signaled by a formulaic setup, which might itself, in turn, become the subject of a meta-joke (*A priest, a rabbi, and a minister walk into a bar. Bartender says, "What is this, a joke?"*).

THE JOKE IS sometimes said to have been invented by Palamedes, the hero of Greek legend who outwitted Odysseus on the eve of the

Trojan War. But since this proverbially ingenious fellow is also credited with inventing numbers, the alphabet, lighthouses, dice, and the practice of eating meals at regular intervals, the claim should perhaps be taken with a grain of salt. In the Athens of Demosthenes, there was a comedians' club called the Group of Sixty, which met in the Temple of Heracles to trade wisecracks, and it is said that Philip of Macedon paid handsomely to have their jokes written down; but the volume, if it ever existed, has been lost. On the Roman side, Plautus refers to jestbooks in a couple of his plays, while Suetonius tells us that Melissus, a favorite professor of the emperor Augustus, compiled no fewer than 150 joke anthologies. Despite this, only a single jokebook survives from ancient times: the *Philogelos*, or "Laughter-Lover," a collection in Greek that was probably put together in the fourth or fifth century A.D. It contains 264 items, several of which appear twice, in slightly different form. This suggests that the volume is

Palamedes. *A Greek hero of the Trojan War, he is credited with inventing the joke—also numbers, money, chess, the alphabet, and the lighthouse, along with breakfast, lunch, and dinner. He was ultimately stoned to death.*

Philip the Great of Macedon (382–336 B.C.).
He paid handsomely to have the first jokebook
compiled; but, alas, it is lost.

not one jokebook but two combined, a hunch borne out by the fact that it is attributed to two authors, Hierocles and Philagrius, although joint authorship was rare at the time. Virtually nothing is known about either man; there is some scholarly speculation that the Hierocles in question was a fifth-century Alexandrian philosopher of that name who was once publicly flogged in Constantinople for paganism, which, as one classicist has observed, "might have given him a taste for mordant wit."

The jokes in the *Philogelos* are spare and pointed. ("'How shall I cut your hair?' a talkative barber asked a wag. 'In silence!'") They take on a gallery of stock characters: the drunk, the miser, the braggart, the sex-starved woman, and the man with bad breath, as well as a classic type known as the *scholastikos*, variously translated as "pedant," "absent-minded professor," or "egghead." ("An egghead was on a sea voyage when a big storm blew up, causing his slaves to weep in

11

Lekythos. *A Greek vessel used to store olive oil, it was inexplicably funny to ancient audiences, as was lettuce.*

terror. 'Don't cry,' he consoled them, 'I have freed you all in my will.'")

Some of the *Philogelos* jokes are now more cryptic than funny, perhaps because of lost undertones. A couple of jokes about lettuce, for example, might have struck a Roman audience as hilarious, given their belief that lettuce leaves, variously, promoted or impeded sexual function. Similarly "An egghead asked his father how much a five-liter flask holds" may have come across to an ancient audience as a double entendre, since some scholars believe that the Greek word for "flask," *lekythos*, was slang for "penis" in Aristophanes.

But others, like no. 263 (lifted from Plutarch), would not be out of place at a Friars Club meeting: "'I had your wife for nothing,' someone sneered at a wag. 'More fool you. I'm her husband, I have to have the ugly bitch. You don't.'" The most haunting joke in the *Philogelos*, however, is no. 114, about a resident of Abdera, a Greek town whose citizens were renowned for their foolishness: "Seeing a eunuch, an Abderite asked him how many children he had. The eunuch replied that he had none, since he lacked the means of reproduction. Retorted the Abderite . . ." The rest is missing from the surviving text, which goes to show the strange potency of unheard punch lines.

THE *Philogelos* was misplaced during the Dark Ages, and with it, seemingly, the art of the joke. Sophisticated humor was kept alive in the Arab world, where the more leisurely folktale was cultivated. During the centuries of Arab conquest, folktales from the Levant, many of them satirical or erotic, made their way through Spain and Italy. An Arab tale about a wife who is pleasured by her lover while her duped husband watches uncomprehendingly from a tree, for instance, is one of several that later show up in Boccaccio's *Decameron*. Once in Europe, the folktale began to cleave in two. On the one hand, with the invention of printing and the rise of literacy, it grew longer, filling out into the chivalric romance and, ultimately, the novel. On the other hand, as the pace of urban life quickened, it got shorter in its oral form, shedding details and growing more formulaic as it condensed into the humorous anecdote. It was in the early Renaissance that the art of the joke was reborn, and the midwife was a man called Poggio.

POGGIO BRACCIOLINI (1380–1459) was one of the most colorful and versatile of the Italian humanists. A secretary to eight popes over a half century, he fathered fourteen children with a mistress before taking, at the age of fifty-five, a beautiful eighteen-year-old bride, who bore him another six children. His career coincided with a turbulent era in church history. During the decades-

Poggio Bracciolini (1380–1459). *Papal secretary and Renaissance humanist, he ran the "fib factory" at the Vatican when he wasn't fathering children by his numerous mistresses.*

long split known as the Western Schism, there were two and sometimes three competing popes, and church councils had to be called to restore unity. Poggio was a passionate bibliophile, and he profited from the disorder, traveling throughout Europe in search of lost works of ancient literature. From the dungeons of remote medieval monasteries he rescued precious manuscripts that had been rotting into oblivion, and laboriously deciphered and copied them. It is thanks to him that we have Lucretius's *De Rerum Natura* and Quintilian's *Institutio Oratoria*, as well as many of the orations of Cicero, the architectural writings of Vitruvius, and Apicius's works on cooking.

Not only was Poggio the greatest book-hunter of his era; he also wielded one of its wickedest pens, satirizing the vices of the clergy and lambasting rival scholars in his Ciceronian Latin. "In his invective he displayed such vehemence that the whole world was afraid of him," a contemporary observed. A skilled calligrapher, Poggio invented

17

the prototype of the roman font. As chancellor of the Republic of Florence after his retirement from the Curia, he became that city's biographer. Yet, for all these accomplishments, Poggio ended up being best known for a book of jokes.

The *Liber Facetiarum*, usually called simply the *Facetiae*, was the first volume of its kind to be published in Europe. In this collection of 273 items—jests, bons mots, puns, and humorous anecdotes—the expansive Arab-Italian *novella* can be seen turning into the swift *facezia*. Some of the material had been gathered by Poggio during his travels through Europe; several of the jests have been traced to tales told by Provençal bards in the twelfth and thirteenth centuries. But much of it came out of a sort of joke club in the Vatican called the Bugiale—the "fib factory." Here papal scribes would gather at the end of a tedious day spent drafting bulls, dispensations, and encyclicals to shoot the breeze and tell scandalous stories.

Poggio published his *Facetiae* in 1451, when he

was seventy years old. Soon the volume was being read throughout Europe. Although many of the jokes were about sex and poked fun at the morals of churchmen, not a word of condemnation was heard from the Vatican. Presumably, since the *Facetiae* were in Latin, they could be savored by the clerical class without corrupting the morals of the masses. Later commentators, however, were not so broad-minded. In 1802 the Reverend William Shepherd, the author of the only biography of Poggio in English, expressed his shock that "an apostolic secretary who enjoyed the friendship and esteem of the pontiff, should have published a number of stories which outrage the laws of decency, and put modesty to the blush."

Copies of the *Facetiae* are not easy to come by today. The only thing I could find in the library of New York University was a photocopied facsimile of an 1878 Paris edition that was the first unexpurgated translation of Poggio's book into French (even then, the really bawdy bits were left in Latin). Reading through it, I was struck by the familiarity of the themes. There are fat jokes, drunk jokes, erection jokes, and fart jokes. One joke, about a guy tricked into drinking urine, would not have been out of place in the movie *American Pie*. In Facetia XLVII, a husband asks his wife why, if women and men get equal pleasure out of sex, it is the men who pursue the women rather than vice versa. "It's obvious," the wife says. "We women are always ready to make love, and you men aren't. What good would it do us to solicit you when you're not in the mood?" As jokes go, this is less than sidesplitting, yet the precise reversal of it appears in the American television show *Curb Your Enthusiasm*, when Cheryl, lying in bed with her husband, Larry, asks him why she's the one who always has to initiate sex. It's because we men are always ready to go, he replies—just tap me on the shoulder when you want it!

By modern standards the *Facetiae* are invariably too long, and Poggio has a regrettable tendency to preempt the punch line with an explanation, as in Facetia XXVI: "The abbot of Septimo, an extremely corpulent man, was traveling toward Florence one evening. On the road he asked a peasant, 'Do you think I'll be able to make it through the city gate?' He was talking about whether he would be able to make it to the city before the gates were closed. The peasant, jesting on the abbot's fatness, said, 'Why, if a cart of hay can make it through, you can, too!'" In XLIV, a friar preaching against adultery concluded by declaring, "It is such an abominable sin that I would rather sleep with ten virgins than a single married woman"—to which Poggio adds, "Many who heard him felt the same way." Sometimes you get a moral in place of a punch line. In CXXXVII, a shaven-headed woman, chided for not covering her head in public, lifts her skirts in an attempt to hide her baldness, thereby exposing her rear end. "This is directed to those who, to correct a light fault, commit a graver one," Poggio informs us. The jests about women too often turn on the monotonous theme that all their maladies stem from not getting enough sex. Nor are the *Facetiae* often very funny, at least when abstracted from the presumably chucklesome atmosphere of the Bugiale and set down in cold print. Nonetheless, by collecting and publishing it, Poggio set the precedent for a slew of later jestbooks, most of which shamelessly plundered his.

WILLIAM CAXTON, England's first printer of books, padded his own translation of Aesop, in 1484, with a sampling of Poggio's jokes, thus creating the earliest jestbook in English. By Shakespeare's time jestbooks had become extremely

*In the Renaissance, medical maladies were
thought to result from not getting enough sex.
Is that funny?*

popular. "I had my good wit out of the 'Hundred Merry Tales,'" the razor-tongued Beatrice declares in *Much Ado About Nothing*, referring to a popular collection of the day. Many of the items in these Tudor and Elizabethan jestbooks are artlessly scatological; for example, "What is the most cleanliest leaf among all other leaves? It is holly leaves, for nobody will wipe his arse with them." Many more are scarcely jokes at all. Instead of racing toward a punch line, they simply describe some prank, typically played by a wife on her husband, or illustrate a moral. (Preachers frequently inserted jests into sermons to keep their congregations from falling asleep.)

Another nudge was needed to finish what Poggio had started: the making of the humorous tale into the joke. It came at the beginning of the seventeenth century, when—possibly because of a confusion with another classical writer called Hierocles—twenty-eight of the *Philogelos* jokes were appended to an edition of his *Commentary*

Beatrice. *The razor-tongued comedienne of*
Shakespeare's Much Ado About Nothing,
she stole her best material from a jokebook.

THE LATE MR. JOSEPH MILLER.

Joe Miller (1684–1738). *This notoriously gloomy English actor's name became a byword for a stale joke.*

on the Golden Words of Pythagoras. The jokes were soon circulating in print throughout Europe.

Thanks to the popularity of the rediscovered *Philogelos* jokes, English humor got shorter and punchier—that is to say, jokier. The change shows up in *Joe Miller's Jests*, the most enduringly popular of the new generation of jokebooks that began to flourish in the Georgian era. (The eponymous Joe Miller, as it happens, was a notoriously gloomy London stage actor; the collection was put together a year after his death by a hack writer, who no doubt intended the title as a joke.) First published in 1739, it went through so many editions that a "Joe Miller" came to mean a stale joke.

The original edition of *Joe Miller's Jests* contained everything from jokes about the fractured logic of Irishmen and bad breath ("A Lady being asked how she liked a Gentleman's Singing, who had a very *stinking* Breath, the Words are good, said she, but the *Air* is intolerable") to bawdy plays on the word "cock" and ribaldry at the expense of loose women ("A Gentleman said of a young Wench who constantly ply'd about the *Temple*, that if she had as much Law in her *Head*, as she had in her *Tail*, she would be one of the ablest *Counsel* in *England*"). The bluer material, however, did not survive the subsequent wave of prudery in Anglo-Saxon culture. In the early nineteenth century, around the time that Thomas Bowdler removed the indelicate bits from Shakespeare, jokebooks also got cleaned up. Little of Poggio could have made it into the expurgated columns of humor magazines like *Punch*. But the dirty joke lived on in oral culture until it was restored to print, in all its repulsive splendor, by Gershon Legman in the 1960s.

LEGMAN, I NOTICED in my decrepit copy of *Rationale of the Dirty Joke*, had dedicated the

volume "To the *Manes* [shade] of Poggio Bracciolini, Lover of Books, Folk-Humor, and Women."
Did he feel some deep affinity with the mischie-
vous Italian humanist? When I mentioned Legman's name in New York literary circles, people
who knew of him—he seems to have left behind
a cult following—would tell me the most out-
landish things: that he created the sixties slogan
Make Love, Not War; that he had an affair with
Anaïs Nin and enlisted her help to write dollar-
a-page pornography to order for a rich Oklahoma
"collector"; that he was behind the invention of
the vibrating dildo; that he introduced origami
to the West; that he had been the editor of an
oddball psychoanalytic quarterly called *Neurotica*;
that he left the United States to escape govern-
ment persecution, taking refuge in a hill town on
the French Riviera, where he lived a hand-to-
mouth existence in a dilapidated castle that had
once belonged to the Knights Templar.

On investigation most of this turned out to be

at least partly true. (We have to take Legman's own word on the dildo and on Make Love, Not War, which he claims to have coined in a lecture at Ohio University in 1963.) Legman was born in 1917 into a Jewish family in the coal country of Pennsylvania. He started collecting jokes early, clipping them from magazines and filing them by theme. After high school he went to New York, where he educated himself in several languages; his university, he said, was the New York Public Library. At the age of twenty-three, he published his first book, *Oragenitalism*, under the pseudonym Roger-Maxe de la Glannège (an anagram of his given name, George Alexander Legman). It bore the subtitle "An Encyclopaedic Outline of Oral Technique in Genital Excitation, Part I, Cunnilinctus." (Legman later explained that he lacked the courage to do the research for fellatio.) At the time, writing a treatise on oral sex was deemed as dangerous as political sedition. When his publisher's office was raided, Legman briefly

Gershon Legman (1917–99). *The indefatigable
encyclopedist of the dirty joke and a man
considered dangerous by the FBI, he coined the
phrase "Make Love, Not War," invented the
vibrating dildo, and introduced origami
to the West.*

fled the state. On his return to New York, he worked as an erotic-book hunter for the sexologist Alfred Kinsey and inhabited the disreputable fringes of the city's literary world, where smut-peddlers were sometimes indistinguishable from avant-garde publishers of Joyce, Lawrence, and Henry Miller.

Legman, however, was more of a moralist than a pornographer. In the late 1940s he wrote *Love and Death*, a fierce polemic, which argued that violence was the true pornography. Why, he asked, should children be exposed to relentless depictions of violence but shielded from those of lovemaking? "At least sex is normal," he wrote. "Is murder?" Legman published the book himself, mailing copies to customers from his three-room cottage in the Bronx. Although *Love and Death* was a tirade against censorship, not a piece of erotica, the United States Postal Service authorities accused its author-publisher of sending "indecent, vulgar and obscene materials" through the mail, and cut off his deliveries. Disgusted, Legman left the country, with his wife, for France. They bought a small piece of land on the Riviera with an olive grove and an old building (which was indeed on the site of a Knights Templar castle) that became a repository for his vast collection of rare volumes and his crates of index cards covered with limericks, jokes, and what he called "pissoir epigraphs."

Legman was a handsome man, five feet nine inches tall (according to his FBI file), with thick dark hair, blue eyes, and a strong nose. Because of chronic poverty, he was typically dressed in threadbare clothes with a length of rope for a belt. Friends describe him as tetchy and difficult, but exhilarating to be around. Academics were put off by this autodidact from the murky demimonde, whose rambling prose was full of marginal jeremiads. Legman, in turn, was disdainful of folklorists with PhDs, whom he called "Phudniks" and "cacademics." Yet, by freely making available to them materials that academic journals were afraid to publish, he helped establish erotic folklore as a respectable subject for scholarly study.

READING THROUGH Legman's vast compilation of dirty jokes is a punishing experience, like being trapped in the men's room of a Greyhound bus station of the 1950s. And the jokes in *Rationale of the Dirty Joke* are what Legman deemed the "clean" dirty jokes, arranged by such relatively innocent themes as "the nervous bride," "phallic brag," and "water wit." In 1975 he published a second fat volume, *No Laughing Matter*, which contained the "dirty" dirty jokes—nearly a thousand pages of jokes about anal sadism, venereal disease, and worse. It was, the author tells us, "a very much harder book to write, though many readers have written to tell me that they '*missed the fag-jokes*' or '*Where the hell are the shit jokes?*'

or were disappointed in the First Series because they did not find their favorite jokes there, and that *'The dirtiest jokes are the funniest.'* I am not sure this is true." But Legman's avowed purpose was not to amuse the reader or furnish him with material for the locker room; he saw his work as a serious psychoanalytic study, one that would disclose the "infinite aggressions" behind jokes, mainly of men against women. For Legman, telling a dirty joke was tantamount to verbal rape.

Legman spent three and a half decades collecting the jokes in these volumes—transcribing some sixty thousand variants on index cards, arranging them by type and motif, and tracing them from country to country and culture to culture, back to the time of Poggio and beyond. They were culled not only from written sources but also from the field: parlor, beer joint, bedroom, and public lavatory. (Many of the jokes are tagged by year and place of discovery: "Idaho 1932," "Penna. 1949.") The result was, by his own account, a vast "decorative showcase" of anxiety, repression, and neurosis, a magnum opus written "almost as often in tears as in laughter." What drove him to this singular labor? According to one friend, he saw himself "as the keeper of the deepest subcellar in the burning Alexandria Library of the age; the subcellar of our secret desires, which no one else was raising so much as a finger to preserve." But Legman must have suspected that he also had a subconscious stake in his massive dirty-joke project. As a lay analyst he believed that "jokes are essentially an unveiling of the joke-teller's own neuroses and compulsions, and his guilts about these." This is a man, after all, whose unpublished autobiography bears the title "Peregrine Penis."

THERE ARE some joke fanatics, however, who are of such an evidently sunny cast that they escape all taint of neurosis. One of these, possibly the most prodigious joke collector of all time, was Nat Schmulowitz (1889–1966). The son of Polish immigrants who ran a speakeasy and nickelodeon in San Francisco, Schmulowitz worked his way through law school. In the early nineteen-twenties, he rose to national fame when he defended the silent-movie comedian Roscoe "Fatty" Arbuckle in one of the most sensational trials of that century. (Arbuckle had been accused of murdering a young starlet in the course of a drunken orgy; after three trials he was acquitted.) Schmulowitz also had Jack Dempsey and Howard Hughes as clients, and he numbered among his friends such Hollywood stars as Buster Keaton and Mary Pickford, whom he would entertain at his summer estate, Smilin' Thru (named after the 1941 Hollywood movie).

Shmulowitz's consuming hobby was collecting humorous ephemera. It all began when he noticed, while reading *Much Ado About Nothing*, Beatrice's reference to the *Hundred Merry Tales*.

Nat Schmulowitz (1889–1966). *A heroic collector of humorous ephemera, he was not particularly funny himself. As a defense attorney, however, he did get Fatty Arbuckle acquitted of murdering a starlet in the course of a drunken orgy.*

Schmulowitz tracked down the sole extant copy of this Elizabethan jestbook in the Royal Library of Göttingen, and he obtained a rare facsimile from a London book dealer. Thereafter he spent his spare moments scouring book catalogs and traveling the globe in search of similarly perishable volumes. "It's a disease," he said, "a wonderful, wonderful disease!" The San Francisco penthouse where Schmulowitz lived with his mother and maiden sister filled up with volumes spanning five centuries and dozens of languages—everything from editions of Poggio's *Facetiae* to issues of *Mad* magazine. On April Fool's Day, 1947, he began to give his collection to the San Francisco Public Library, continuing his donations at the rate of up to a hundred volumes a month over the next two decades. Today they form the core of the Schmulowitz Collection of Wit and Humor, possibly the largest collection of its kind in the world. (Its only rival is the House of Humor and Satire in Gabrovo, Bulgaria, of all places.)

A short, stout, balding man, Schmulowitz was known for his warmth and modesty. He was not especially funny himself, according to his niece, Geraldine Weill Levine, but "he would come up with a good pun now and then." He adored such comedians as Milton Berle, Phyllis Diller, and Sid Caesar, giving them the run of his collection of humor. Schmulowitz was a tireless advocate of the power of jokes, which he called "the small change of history." In a speech before the judges of the Ninth Judicial Circuit, "Liberty, Laughter and the Law," he spoke ringingly of how jokes have "detected and exposed the impostor and have saved man from the oppression of false leaders." The enormous archive of printed drollery that he bequeathed to the San Francisco Public Library was meant to stand as a testament to his conviction that "without humor, we are doomed."

TALKING TO one of the librarians who today over-
see the Schmulowitz Collection, which is open to
the public, I was mildly surprised to learn that
the most frequently requested item was *Flagellation and the Flagellants: A History of the Rod in
All Countries*, a 1910 book whose frontispiece
shows "the beautiful Madame LaPuchin" having her exposed derrière soundly whipped. Does
this qualify as humor? Well, jokes *are* a medium
for fantasizing about what must be avoided in
reality, a way of laughing off our cruel, irratio-
nal, and aggressive instincts. An enthusiasm
for a certain species of joke can be revealing in
ways the enthusiast might not fully appreciate.
Take the dead-baby jokes that were popular in
the United States in the 1960s (*What's red and
swings? A baby on a meat hook*, and so on). If
you were one of the teenagers who used to tell
such jokes, it might conceivably have had something to do with murderous impulses arising
from sibling rivalry. Even parents could see the

41

Madame LaPuchin in ecstasy. *The most frequently requested item in the world's largest library of humor concerns the practice of flagellation.*

humor; after all, babies are such a lot of bother. Although "sick jokes" of this sort lay outside the clinical purview of Gershon Legman, who was exclusively interested in sex and scatology, he did make a slightly puzzled reference to them in the introduction to his dirty-joke book, mentioning a certain "Dr. Dundes" as an authority.

ALAN DUNDES, a folklorist at the University of California at Berkeley, was reverentially known there as the "Joke Professor." Until his death in 2005—he collapsed of a heart attack in the classroom, a joke on his lips—Dundes was the academy's most assiduous collector of jokes, the heir to Poggio, Legman, and Schmulowitz. In his long career he produced several analytical collections of humor, notably *Cracking Jokes* (1987). He also wrote or coauthored many articles in folklore journals on specific joke themes, with titles like "Here I Sit: A Study of American Latrinalia" (toilet jokes); "Arse Longa, Vita Brevis" (AIDS jokes); "First Prize: Fifteen Years" (dissident jokes from Eastern Europe—the title is the punch line to the setup "Did you hear about the joke contest in Bucharest?"); and even a study of jokes about the sex-addled politician Gary Hart, "Six Inches from the Presidency"—which, he proudly informed me when I first met him on a sunny day in mellow Berkeley, had just been translated into Russian.

As a boy growing up in the suburbs of New York City, Dundes was fascinated with jokes. His father, an attorney, would return home from the city each evening with a few jokes he had picked up while playing bridge on the commuter train out of Grand Central, and tell them over dinner. As a graduate student at Yale, Dundes took a course in poetry with Cleanth Brooks and became interested in Yeats's use of Celtic mythology. This led him to the study of folklore, then an academically marginal field. In 1962, he obtained his PhD from Indiana University, where, as a course requirement, candidates had to submit a hundred items of folklore that they had collected and analyzed. Dundes turned in a lot of jokes.

"Before then, it had never occurred to me to analyze the jokes I collected," Dundes told me. "But Vladimir Propp's *Morphology of the Folktale* had just come out in English"—he was referring to the 1928 work that identified thirty-one narrative elements that constitute the underlying structure of Russian fairy tales—"and I thought, Hey, this is a great methodology for jokes. So I was early to hop on the structuralist bandwagon." But Dundes was also a Freudian, and remained one to his death, "even in these days of Freud bashing." Freud himself was an industrious collector of Jewish jokes and considered them deeply significant. Although Freud's collection was most likely destroyed in one of his periodic manuscript-burning sessions, some two hundred jokes, tales, puns, and riddles appear in his 1905 book *Jokes and Their Relation to the Unconscious*. Dundes was greatly influenced by this seminal work, which likens jokes to dreams. (Both involve the condensation and displacement of meanings, the representation of things by their opposites, the triumph of fallacy over logic—all to outwit the inner censor.) "Some people believe jokes and nursery rhymes and fairy tales are just harmless little stories that don't mean anything," Dundes told me. "But they're not meaningless. And they're not necessarily harmless, either."

To illustrate the point, Dundes cited an apparently gentle and innocuous joke cycle that was popular in the 1960s: the elephant joke. It is no accident that elephant jokes appeared around the beginning of the civil rights movement, he said. Consider the parallels between the elephant and the white stereotype of the black: the association with the jungle, the potential for violence, the idea of unusually large genitals and corresponding sexual capacity. "You

Alan Dundes (1934–2005). *The revered "joke
professor" of Berkeley, he saw the sinister side
of elephant jokes.*

can see this even in the seemingly most nonsensi-
cal jokes," he said. "*Why did the elephant sit on the
marshmallow? So he wouldn't fall into the cocoa.* That
reflects the white person's fear of blacks moving
into his neighborhood—they're trying to sit on the
white oasis in the chocolate, so to speak. This joke
was being told at a time when even liberals felt anx-
ious about the effects of integration." I confessed to
Dundes that I found his interpretation a tad, well,
oversubtle. But he insisted that there was plenty of
anecdotal data in its favor. "When a psychiatrist
friend of mine asked his black secretary if she knew
any elephant jokes, she said, 'Why would *we* tell
them? They're *about* us.'"

I COULD NOT resist posing the tiresome but still
mysterious question: Where do jokes come from?
"There are two classic theories about the origin
of jokes," Dundes said. "One is that they come

from stockbrokers, who have time on their hands between sales and a communications network to send jokes around. The other theory is that they are made up by prisoners, who have a lot of spare time and a captive audience." He added, "Lately these two theories have merged."

But the romantic ideal of individual creation seems inadequate when it comes to jokes. "The classic ones get told over and over again in updated dress," Dundes noted. "A good example is one that I first heard about Richard Nixon. So Nixon's taking a walk around the White House grounds one winter day when he comes across the words 'I hate Tricky Dick' written in urine in the snow. He tells the Secret Service to investigate. A week later, they come back to him and say, 'Well, Mr. President, we've analyzed the urine, and it turns out to be Secretary Kissinger's. But we've also analyzed the handwriting, and it's the First Lady's.'" Dundes heard the same joke during the Clinton years, with Kissinger and Pat Nixon replaced by Al Gore and Hillary, or even Chelsea. Indeed, versions of it go back to the Ozark mountain culture of the 1890s. "People on the Internet today have no idea that the jokes they're trading are hundreds of years old," he said.

᠆᠊ᠵᡟᡖ᠊᠆

FOLKLORISTS ARE fond of the idea that jokes don't get invented; they evolve. As Legman put it, "*Nobody* ever tells jokes for the first time." Really new jokes, especially of the coarser variety, are supposed to be a rarity. While the claim may be exaggerated, there is more truth to it than one might think. A few years ago, a schoolboy told me a joke from a genre that is hugely popular with children, the fart joke: "Why do farts smell? So deaf people can enjoy them too!" Reading though the ancient jokes in the *Philogelos*, I was a little surprised to come across essentially the same joke in no. 241: "A fool broke wind whilst in bed with

Queen Elizabeth I (1533–1603).
She had forgott the Fart.

a deaf person. When the latter caught the smell and began to complain, the fool said, 'Come on, how could you hear it if you are supposed to be deaf?'" Another specimen in this genre, known as *the fortunate fart* (because the person guilty of the gastric lapse eventually benefits as a result), can be traced back through Mark Twain to John Aubrey, who, in his brief life of Edward de Vere, an Elizabethan earl and courtier, relates the following: "This Earle of Oxford, making of his low obeisance to Queen Elizabeth, happened to let a Fart, at which he was so abashed and ashamed that he went to Travell, 7 yeares. On his returne the Queen welcomed him home, and sayd, My Lord, I had forgott the Fart." There is a still earlier version of this low jest in the *Arabian Nights* story, "How Abu Hassan Brake Wind."

In another contemporary joke, sent to me by a Wall Street trader, the different parts of the body argue about which of them is the most important. The argument is finally won by the anus, who

points out that if it chooses to cease functioning
everyone else gets shut down. Punch line: The
boss is an asshole! This joke, I was slightly flab-
bergasted to discover, has an antecedent in the
New Testament; specifically, in the First Epistle
to the Corinthians, wherein, after considering the
relative merits of the different body parts, Paul
concludes that "God has so adjusted the body,
giving the greater honor to the inferior part"—a
part which, despite its usefulness, the epistle had
earlier deemed "unpresentable."

Or take this chestnut, current in mid-twentieth-
century America, about an impecunious couple
who marry for love. Since there is nothing for
breakfast in the morning, the husband instead
has sex with his wife on the kitchen table before
going off to work and also when he returns home
for lunch. Coming back famished in the evening, the husband finds his wife sitting in the
kitchen with her panties down and her feet up
on the oven door. "Just warming up your supper,

darling," she says. This jest can be traced back to a late-eighteenth-century Scottish rhyme called "The Supper Is Na Ready," and from there almost two centuries earlier to a 1618 French collection of libertine poetry ("*Mais le souper n'est pas encore cuit*"), and ultimately to the *Philogelos*: "Said a young man to his randy wife, 'Wife, what shall we do, eat or make love?' 'Whichever you like; there's no bread.'"

That may be the longest joke lineage ever established, reaching back some fifteen centuries. It is the labor of the great joke collectors—a few brilliant, polymathic, and sometimes eccentric men—that has made us aware of such continuities in the nether regions of civilization. Some have piggybacked on the work of earlier collectors; others have added analyses or rhetorical flourishes. But Poggio remains the most important of them, the man who reintroduced the lost classical art of the joke to Western culture.

~·⊰⊱·~

AFTER POGGIO's death the people of Florence entombed him with much pomp in the Church of Santa Croce. Donatello was commissioned to make a statue of him, which was installed in the facade of the Duomo. A century later, in 1569, some alterations were undertaken in the cathedral, and Poggio's statue was removed from its original position and placed in a grouping of the twelve apostles. There the first modern joke collector can be found, timelessly keeping company with martyrs and evangelists.

Part II

PHILOSOPHY

Laughter. *Usually healthful;*
sometimes fatal.

THE TRUE, THE BEAUTIFUL, AND THE
Good—such are the traditional staples of
philosophy. Of this hoary trio, the middle member has proved especially vexing over the centuries. Today, beauty is thought to be too narrow
and old-fashioned a concept to encompass the
qualities in art and nature which give us pleasure.
Philosophers talk instead of "aesthetic value." And
the least problematic way of defining aesthetic
value is in terms of the characteristic response it
elicits in the observer: an "aesthetic experience."

How can you tell when you are having an

aesthetic experience? The bodily symptoms, if any, tend to be subtle. A passage in a Bach fugue may fleetingly give you gooseflesh. A line from Yeats might make you tingle a bit, or cause the little hairs on the back of your neck to stand up in appreciation. But there is one kind of aesthetic experience whose outward expression is grossly palpable. It involves the contraction of some fifteen facial muscles, along with the simultaneous stimulation of the muscles of inspiration and those of expiration, which gives rise to a series of respiratory spasms accompanied by a burst of vowel-based notes. Healthful side effects of this experience are believed to include oxygenation of the blood, reduction in stress hormones, and a bolstering of the immune system through heightened T-cell activity. But if the experience is too intense, cataplexy can set in, leading to muscular collapse and possible injury. In rare cases the consequences are graver still. Anthony Trollope suffered a stroke undergoing this experience while reading a now-forgotten Victorian novel, *Vice Versa*. And, according to tradition, the ancient Greek painter Zeuxis, reacting to the portrait of a hag he had just made, actually died of it.

What I have been describing is, of course, laughter. It is our characteristic response to the aesthetic category of the humorous, the comical, or the funny. This raises an interesting question: What is it about the humorous situation that evokes this response? Why should a certain kind of cerebral activity issue in such a peculiar behavioral reflex, one that serves no obvious evolutionary purpose? As Voltaire mockingly observed in the entry under "Laughter" in his *Dictionnaire philosophique*, "Those who know why this kind of joy that kindles laughter should draw the zygomatic muscle back toward the ears are knowing indeed."

~❧~

WHILE THERE can be laughter without humor—tickling, embarrassment, nitrous oxide, and vengeful exultation have been known to bring it forth—there cannot be humor without laughter. That, at any rate, is what contemporary philosophers think. "The propensity of the state of amusement to issue in laughter is arguably what is essential to its identity," we read under "Humour" in the *Routledge Encyclopedia of Philosophy*. But laughter is physical. You need to have a body to do it. So, if the philosophers are right, purely spiritual beings couldn't really "get" a joke. (Homeric gods, being corporeal, can and do laugh; we are told that Zeus, after his birth, laughed continuously for seven days.)

Mere possession of a body, however, does not guarantee that one will laugh with any frequency. Isaac Newton is reported to have laughed precisely once in his life—when someone asked him what use he saw in Euclid's *Elements*. Joseph Stalin, too, seems to have been somewhat agelastic (from the Greek *a-*, "not," *gelastes*, "laugher"). "Seldom did anyone see Stalin laugh," we read in Marshal Georgy Zhukov's reminiscences. "When he did, it was more like a chuckle, as though to himself." Other reputed agelasts include Jonathan Swift, William Gladstone, Margaret Thatcher, and Supreme Court Justice Ruth Bader Ginsburg. Jesus wept, but did he laugh? That was the core question of Umberto Eco's *The Name of the Rose*. As I was unable to finish the novel, I'm not sure what the answer is, but I do not recall much laughter in the Gospels. "The total absence of humor from the Bible," Alfred North Whitehead once observed, "is one of the most singular things in all literature."

Like love, its only rival as an inner source of pleasure for mankind, laughter bridges the realms of the mental and the physical: So observed the incomparable Max Beerbohm in his 1920 essay

THREE AGELASTS OF NOTE.

Sir Isaac Newton (1642–1727).
He laughed but once in his life, over geometry.

Baruch Spinoza (1632–77).
*He proclaimed that "laughter is
merely pleasure," yet he himself
laughed only when watching
spiders
fight to the death.*

Joseph V. Stalin
(1879–1953).
*The dictator was
a cold audience for
jokes.*

"Laughter." But, Beerbohm noted, whereas love originates in the physical and culminates in the mental, the vector of laughter points in precisely the opposite direction, from the mental to the physical. One might also draw a parallel with sex. The objective in sexual congress, according to the Marquis de Sade, is to elicit involuntary noise-making from your partner—which is precisely the objective of humor, even if the nature of the noisemaking is a bit different.

It is an oft-registered complaint that philosophers do not devote enough attention to laughter and humor. In the *Oxford Companion to Philosophy*, for example, the entry under "Humour" opens, "Although laughter, like language, is often cited as one of the distinguishing features of human beings, philosophers have spent only a small proportion of their time and pages on it and on the allied topic of amusement when compared with the volumes devoted to the philosophy of language." Aperçus can be found here and

there in the philosophical canon. Plato deemed
the proper objects of laughter to be vice and folly.
Aristotle declared the laughable to be a species
of the ugly. Spinoza—who, according his friends,
laughed out loud only when watching his favorite spectacle, that of two spiders fighting to the
death—observed in his *Ethics* that "Laughter is
merely pleasure" and, as such, is "in itself good."
Hobbes, Kant, and Schopenhauer all hazarded
somewhat elliptical theories of humor as asides in
major writings. To find an entire treatise devoted
to laughter and humor, however, you have to go
to a second-rater like the French vitalist philosopher Henri Bergson, who, in his book *Le rire*
(1899), defined the comic as "the encrustation
of the mechanical on the living"—the paradigm
case, disappointingly, being a man slipping on a
banana peel.

There are several reasons why philosophers
might be reluctant to take up the problem of
humor. First there is the general principle that

the more interesting *x* is, the less interesting the philosophy of *x* tends to be, and conversely. (Art is interesting, but the philosophy of art is mostly boring; law is boring, the philosophy of law is pretty interesting.) Then there is the feeling that the secret of something as precious as laughter should not be pried into. Finally, there is the fear that the analysis of amusement is likely to be unamusing—or worse, unintentionally amusing. As Saul Steinberg observed, "Trying to define humor is one of the definitions of humor."

No FIGURE in the philosophical tradition has produced a sustained account of humor and laughter that bears comparison with Sigmund Freud's *Jokes and Their Relation to the Unconscious*. Freud's interest in the problem of humor was not primarily philosophical. Rather, he was specifically attracted to jokes—a subgenre of the

Sigmund Freud (1856–1939).
The psychoanalyst of humor, whose own
favorite jokes betrayed a deep ambivalence
about his Jewish identity.

humorous—because of their many likenesses to dreams. (When Freud's friend and medical collaborator Wilhelm Fliess was reading the proofs of *The Interpretation of Dreams* in the fall of 1899, he complained that the dreams seemed to contain an awful lot of jokes.) In both jokes and dreams, Freud observed, meanings are condensed and displaced, things are represented indirectly or by their opposites, fallacious reasoning trumps logic. Jokes often arise involuntarily, like dreams, and tend to be swiftly forgotten. From these similarities Freud inferred that jokes and dreams share a common origin in the unconscious. Both are essentially means of outwitting our inner "censor." Yet there is a critical difference, Freud insisted. Jokes are meant to be understood; indeed, this is crucial to their success. The meaning of a dream, by contrast, eludes even the dreamer. It is little wonder that one's own dreams are utterly uninteresting to other people (except, perhaps, one's analyst). In a sense, a dream is a failed joke.

Freud was an avid collector of jokes, particularly Jewish jokes, and his book contains 138 specimens, by my count. Some are excellent ("A royal personage was making a tour through his provinces and noticed a man in the crowd who bore a striking resemblance to his own exalted person. He beckoned to him and asked: 'Was your mother at one time in service in the Palace?'—'No, your Highness,' was the reply, 'but my father was.'"). Some are middling ("A Jew noticed the remains of some food in another one's beard. 'I can tell you what you had to eat yesterday.'—'Well, tell me.'—'Lentils, then—.' 'Wrong: that was the day before yesterday.'"). Some are dated—to put it charitably—or perish in translation ("Mr. and Mrs. X live in fairly grand style. Some people think that the husband has earned a lot and so has been able to lay by a bit [*sich etwas zurück-gelegt*]; others again think that the wife has lain back a bit [*sich etwas zurückgelegt*] and so has been able to earn a lot." Freud reckons this "a really diabolically ingenious joke!"). And when it comes to phrasing, Freud is no Henny Youngman; one of his efforts begins, "An impoverished individual borrowed 25 florins from a prosperous acquaintance, with many asseverations of his necessitous circumstances . . ."

In making his idiosyncratic collection of jokes, Freud left himself open to analysis. In 1997 the folklorist Elliott Oring put him on the couch in the book *The Jokes of Sigmund Freud*, concluding that Freud's jokes betrayed a deep ambivalence about his Jewish identity, an ambivalence that could be traced to a childhood episode in which his nurse caught him spitting on the steps. The very impulse to amass jokes, which are usually considered to be relatively worthless and disposable items, can be given a psychosexual explanation. In a 1917 paper on "anal eroticism," Freud offered the following analysis. The infant is confused by his bodily products. His excrement seems to be of some value, since it issues from his body and attracts the interest of his parents (it's the infant's "first gift," Freud says); but this excrement is taken away and disposed of, so it also seems valueless. Gradually the child is weaned away from his normal curiosity in the waste products of his body, via the reality principle, by a series of drier and drier substitutes—mud-pies, sand piles, and so on. Yet, among neurotics, the urge to hoard that which is disposable and of little intrinsic value—old newspapers, coasters, empty beer cans, money—remains. (The identification of gold with feces, according to Freud, is behind such locutions as "filthy rich" and a "shitload of money.") And nothing is more disposable than a joke.

~❧~

PHILOSOPHERS HAVE been less bold than Freud in their quest for a theory of jokes. Some think it's futile even to look for such a theory. Ted Cohen, a distinguished philosopher at the University of Chicago, is one of these. "Every general theory of jokes known to me is wrong," he wrote in his 1999 study, *Jokes*. "Such a monotonic theory always seizes upon one or two kinds of jokes, and misses the other kinds." Perhaps jokes are simply too diverse to have a common denominator. The philosopher Ludwig Wittgenstein once observed that certain concepts were like family resemblances. Members of a family tend to look alike even though, as a group, they may not all share any one facial feature. Some of them might have the same hair and eyes but a different nose, others might have different eyes but the same nose and chin, and so on. Maybe jokes are like that. If so, any philosophical theory that purported to identify the essence of the joke would necessarily distort the concept.

How many kinds of jokes are there? Well, there are topical jokes (*Did you know Nixon had to see* Deep Throat *seven times before he could get it down Pat?*) and perennial jokes (*"How's your wife?" "Compared to what?"*). There are jokes that presuppose a good deal of culture (*Panhandler accosts* a guy on the sidewalk outside a Broadway theater. *The guy declines to give him anything, saying, "'Neither a borrower nor a lender be.'—Shakespeare." Panhandler replies, "'Fuck you!'—Mamet"*) and jokes that are universally appreciated because they require little in the way of specialized knowledge or feelings (*I was so unpopular when I was little, even my imaginary friend played with the kid across the street*).

There are classic jokes (*"Who was that lady I saw you with last night?" "That was no lady, that was my wife"*) that get subjected to hip-hop inversion (*"Who was that ho I saw you with last night?" "That was no ho, that was my bitch"*) and then to philosophical pastiche (*"Oh Socrates, who was that lady I saw you with last night?" "That was no lady, that was Alcibiades"*).

There are jokes about different groups of people, like the Unitarians (*How do you protest when a Unitarian family moves into your neighborhood? You burn a question mark on their lawn*), or the Teamsters (*How do you tell when a Teamster has died?*

The doughnut rolls out of his hand), or rednecks
(*Why do rednecks have sex doggy-style? So they can
both watch NASCAR on TV*). There are even jokes
about castrati, which no one can dismiss as a load
of bollocks.

The "Jewish American Princess," or JAP, is a
particular butt, notably for her shopping habits
and her reluctance to engage in certain sexual
acts. (*Why do JAPs prefer circumcised men? They like
anything with 20 percent off. What do you get when
you cross a JAP with a Mac? A computer that never
goes down.*)

There are jokes about musical instruments,
especially the viola, which seems to be especially
despised in the world of classical music. (*Why did
the chicken cross the road? To get away from the viola
recital.* Or, in a more esoteric vein, *How was the
canon invented? When two violists attempted to play
in unison.*)

There are geographical jokes, including jokes
about all fifty of the American states and, somewhat

redundantly, the Virgin Islands. (*Why is New Jersey called the Garden State? Because there's a Rosenblum on every block. What do a hurricane and a divorce in West Virginia have in common? Somebody's gonna lose a trailer.*) Curiously, Missouri used to be called the "Puke State," although this was not a jocular reference to vomit, but rather a corruption of "Pikes," a western term used for migratory workers coming out of Missouri's Pike County.

There are political jokes, such as Ronald Reagan's definition of liberalism: *If it moves, tax it. If it keeps moving, regulate it. If it stops moving, subsidize it.* The Iraq War has spawned an entire new category of "neocon" jokes, for example, *How many neocons does it take to screw in a lightbulb? None—President Bush has announced that in three months the lightbulb will be able to change itself.* Or, to take a specimen inspired by the brusque manners of Dick Cheney, *How many neocons does it take to screw in a lightbulb? Go fuck yourself!*

There are jokes about national disasters, premised on the dubious notion that comedy equals tragedy plus time (*Why did the space shuttle Challenger blow up? The astronauts were free-basing Tang*). Some of these, oddly, take the form of a child's knock-knock joke (*"Knock knock." "Who's there?" "9-11." "9-11 who?" "YOU SAID YOU'D NEVER FORGET!"*).

There are nice jokes that can be told in any drawing room (*What does a snail say when riding on the back of a turtle? "Whee!"*) And there are naughty jokes that might shock a dowager—like *How do you titillate an ocelot? You oscillate its tits a lot*—reputedly a favorite of George H. W. Bush. Or the one about the lady who flies into Boston eager to enjoy a plate of the fish that city is famous for. "Where can I get scrod?" she demands of the driver as she gets into the cab. "Gee," he replies, "I've never heard it put in the pluperfect subjective before!" Or the one about the successful diet Bill Clinton went on: *He's lost so much weight, now he can see his intern.* Or the one told every year on

Monica Lewinsky's birthday: *Imagine, Monica's thirty years old already! It seems like only yesterday she was crawling around the floor of the Oval Office.* Or the one about how Times Square hookers get into the tax-season spirit around April 15: *For an extra fifty dollars they'll handle your extension.*

There are jokes that are inadvertent as well as jokes that are deliberate—and some that are, paradoxically, both at the same time, such as the London newspaper headline during World War II, BRITISH PUSH BOTTLES UP GERMANS. There are also jokes that simultaneously manage to be both lowly and surreal (*A friend asked me if I wanted a frozen banana. I said, "No, but I want a regular banana later so, yeah!"*).

There are short jokes, some with a single-syllable punch line (*What's brown and sounds like a bell? Dung!*) There is even the rare joke consisting of only two words ("Pretentious? *Moi*?").

Is a one-word joke logically possible? I would propose *Kalamazoo!*, which is, of course, the name of a perfectly worthy city in Michigan. It gets off to a good start, as the consonant *K* is thought by those in the humor business to be intrinsically funny; the set-up (*Ka-la-ma-*) obeys comedy's "Rule of Three"; and the punch line (*zoo!*) abruptly shifts, via the sibilant *z*, to the silliest phoneme in the English language.

Finally, as we all know, there are long jokes, jokes that would swell a footnote to monstrous proportions.*

Cruising on Fifth Avenue one day, a taxi is hailed by a man standing on the corner. Entering the cab, the man says, "Take me to the Palmer House."

"The Palmer House?" says the cabbie. "That's in Chicago."

"I know," says his fare. "That's where I want to go."

"I'll drive you to Kennedy," says the cabbie. "You can fly."

"I'm afraid of flying."

"Then I'll drive you over to Grand Central and you can take the train."

"No, the train takes too long and besides, then I'd have to get from Union Station to the Palmer House."

"If I drove you all the way to Chicago it would cost a fortune. Twice a fortune, because you'd have to pay for me to deadhead back to New York."

Could any theory make sense of even this little sampling of jokes? There are three competing traditions, all a bit moldy, that purport to explain how humor works.

The "superiority theory"—propounded in various forms by Plato, Hobbes, and Bergson—locates

---

"That's okay. I can afford it. Here's a few hundred dollars now. I'll pay the rest when we get there."

With no further argument to make, the cabbie drives out of Manhattan into New Jersey and then connects with the Pennsylvania Turnpike, thence to the Ohio Turnpike, the Indiana Turnpike, and finally the Skyway into Chicago. He takes Stony Island to Fifty-seventh Street, where he turns onto Lake Shore Drive. He drives north as far as Congress, cuts over to Michigan Avenue, and goes north again until he can pull over to Wabash, drives back one block south, and screeches to a stop in front of the Wabash entrance to the Palmer House—after two days and one night of nonstop driving.

The passenger peers at the meter, gives the cabbie several hundred dollars to cover the fare and a decent tip, and then opens the door to step onto the sidewalk.

Before anyone can close the door, two women who have been standing at the curb slide into the backseat of the cab. One of the women says, "We want to go to an address on Flatbush Avenue."

"Uh-uh, lady," says the cabbie. "I don't go to Brooklyn."

"Sorry, lady, I don't go to Brooklyn."

the essence of humor in the "sudden glory" (Hobbes) we feel when, say, we see Bill Gates get hit in the face with a custard pie. According to this theory all humor is at root mockery and derision, all laughter a slightly spiritualized snarl.

The "incongruity theory," held by Pascal, Kant, and Schopenhauer, says that humor arises when the decorous and logical abruptly dissolves into the low and absurd. "Do you believe in clubs for small children?" W. C. Fields is asked. "Only when kindness fails," he replies.

Why either of these perceptions—superiority or incongruity—should call forth a bout of cackling and chest heaving remains far from obvious. It is an advantage of the third theory, the "relief theory," that it at least tries to explain the causal link between humor and laughter. In Freud's version, the laughable—ideally a naughty joke—liberates the laugher from inhibitions about forbidden thoughts and feelings. The result is a discharge of nervous energy through the facial and respiratory muscles—a noisy outburst that, not incidentally, serves to distract the inner censor from what is going on.

⌁

FOR A SCIENTIST, choosing among competing theories generally means looking at how well they fit the data. And when the theories are about humor, jokes supply plenty of data. The superiority theory is well suited to jokes involving misfortune and deformity (*How did Helen Keller burn her fingers? She tried to read a waffle iron*), jokes about drunkards and henpecked husbands and lawyers, jokes about despised ethnic and racial groups. It may well explain the pleasure some take in a joke like this:

> *Angry guy walks into a bar, orders a drink, says to the bartender, "All agents are assholes."*

> *Guy sitting at the end of the bar says, "Just a min-*
> *ute, I resent that."*
> *"Why? You an agent?"*
> *"No. I'm an asshole."*

With a bit of stretching the superiority theory can be made to cover almost all kinds of jokes, even those where contempt for the object of amusement gives way to sympathy. Superiority might be interpreted as a sort of godlike perspective upon human affairs, or upon the universe itself. (Max Beerbohm, debarking at the Port of New York, was asked by a reporter what he thought of the Statue of Liberty. "It is very vulgar," Beerbohm said. "It must come down.")

But what of the pun, widely and perhaps justly regarded as the lowest form of humor? (Vladimir Nabokov, when told by a professor of English that a nun who was auditing one of the professor's classes had complained that two students in the back of the classroom were "spooning"

"It is very vulgar," said Max Beerbohm.
"It must come down."

during a lecture: "You should have said, 'Sister, you're lucky they weren't forking.'") Well, one might say that in wordplay we are enjoying our superiority to language or reason. But now the superiority theory has become elastic to the point of meaninglessness.

The relief theory of humor has similar problems in fitting the data. It works well enough for what Freud called "tendentious" jokes—the smutty, nasty, blasphemous kind. Such jokes quite obviously express forbidden impulses of an aggressive or sexual nature. The relief theory works less well for jokes based on sheer nonsense. Such "innocent" jokes, Freud claimed, also serve to overcome an inhibition: the adult inhibition against play. By freeing us momentarily from the bondage of logic and reality, they transport us back to the euphoric mood of childhood, when "we were accustomed to deal with our psychical work in general with a small expenditure of energy" and "we had no need of humor to make us feel happy in our life."

But even "innocent" jokes are not entirely innocent, Freud claimed, since the urge to make them
"may be equated with exhibitionism in the sexual
field."

The pleasure of a tendentious joke, according to the Freudian account, arises from the sat-
isfaction of an instinct, either lustful or hostile,
that is usually blocked; whereas the pleasure of
an innocent joke consists in the enjoyment of
the art of joke making for its own sake ("strictly
speaking, we do not know what we are laughing
at"). Because of these different sources of pleasure, Freud thought, tendentious jokes tended to
get bigger laughs than innocent ones. But is this
really true? Back in the nineties *Esquire* magazine
published a list of what the editors and their con-
sultants (who included Dick Cavett, Al Franken,
and David Brenner) deemed "the seventy-five
funniest jokes of all time." The joke that ranked
number one (credited to Garry Shandling) was:
I went to my doctor and told him, "My penis is

burning." He said, "That means somebody is talking about it." This is ribald enough, but it is hardly tendentious in Freud's sense, since the form of the joke makes no attempt to beguile the inner censor; the forbidden material is already present in the setup. (Compare a joke that was told to me by an angelic-looking seventh-grader at a Catholic girls' school where I once taught: "Mr. Holt, what's better than roses on a piano? Tulips on an organ.") Perhaps the most amusing joke near the top of the *Esquire* ranking (number eight, to be precise) was, as it happens, the very soul of innocence: *Skeleton walks into a bar and says, "Give me a beer and a mop."*

Freud's theory has another empirical shortcoming. If the pleasure we derive from jokes comes from the release of psychic energy used to inhibit aggressive and sexual impulses, then it follows that the people who laugh the hardest at malicious jokes should be the ones who most deeply bury their aggressive tendencies.

By the same token, the people who laugh the
hardest at lewd jokes should be the ones who are
the most sexually repressed. But in practice the
opposite seems to be the case. Research by the
late British psychologist Hans Eysenck suggests
that the people who get the biggest kick out of
aggressive/sexual jokes are generally the ones
least inhibited about displaying their impulses.
On the other hand, the Freudian theory may
help account for national tastes in dirty jokes:
the proverbial popularity of anal jokes among
the Dutch and Germans, of homosexual jokes
among the English, of oral-genital jokes among
Americans, and of jokes about cuckoldry and
the more pleasant aspects of seduction among
the French—who are, presumably, the least
repressed. (French children, for dark reasons of
their own, seem to have a special fondness for
jokes about a fantastic creature called the *zizi
tordu*, or "twisted penis.")

Garry Shandling (*fl. circa* 1990).
This now-forgotten American comedian
invented a joke that was voted the funniest
of all time by a panel of experts. It
concerned his penis.

❦

OF THE THREE theories of humor, it is the incongruity theory that is taken most seriously by philosophers today. It too, however, is open to objections. Why should incongruity be a source of pleasure? Shouldn't the asymmetrical, the disorderly, and the absurd cause bewilderment and anxiety in rational creatures like ourselves, not merriment? The nineteenth-century philosopher Alexander Bain observed:

> There are many incongruities that may produce anything but a laugh. A decrepit man under a heavy burden, five loaves and two fishes among a multitude, and all unfitness and gross disproportion; an instrument out of tune, a fly in ointment, snow in May, Archimedes studying geometry in a siege, and all discordant things; a wolf in sheep's clothing, a breach of bargain, and falsehood

in general; the multitude taking the law into their own hands, and everything of the nature of disorder; a corpse at a feast, parental cruelty, filial ingratitude, and whatever is unnatural; the entire catalogue of vanities given by Solomon—are all incongruous, but they cause feelings of pain, anger, sadness, loathing, rather than mirth.

(Bain was a dour Victorian Scotsman, with little capacity for the darker forms of humor; but one sees what he is getting at.) Some forms of incongruity, moreover, have aesthetic value without being the least bit funny: the ironies of *Oedipus Rex*, for example, or the dissonances in Mozart's String Quartet in C major.

Even if not all incongruities are funny, nearly everything that is funny does seem to contain an incongruity of one sort or another. For Kant the incongruity in a joke was between the "something" of the setup and the anticlimactic "nothing" of

Immanuel Kant (1724–1804). *The great German philosopher pioneered the incongruity theory of humor, but instead of telling jokes to his friends he preferred to share with them his bodily complaints, which included headaches and chronic constipation.*

the punch line; the ludicrous effect arises "from the sudden transformation of a strained expectation into nothing." (In the *Critique of Judgment*, Kant illustrates the point with a story: An Indian who is dining with an Englishman looks astonished when a bottle of ale is opened and the contents come gushing out in a wave of froth. "Well, what is so wonderful in that?" asks the Englishman. "Oh, I'm not surprised at its getting out," replies the Indian, "but at how you ever managed to get it all in.") Schopenhauer thought that at the core of every joke was a sophistical syllogism. But some jokes simply defy syllogistic analysis. (Lily Tomlin: "When I was young I always wanted to be somebody. Now I wish I had been more specific.")

IS IT POSSIBLE to find any jokes that do not contain some sort of incongruity? Earl Butz, secretary of agriculture during the Nixon and Ford administrations, lost his job in 1976 over one such joke. Butz was overheard on a commercial flight saying that "the only thing coloreds are looking for in life are a tight pussy, loose shoes, and a warm place to shit." (When this story broke, the *Washington Post* printed the remark verbatim, whereas the *New York Times* resorted to the prim periphrasis of "satisfying sex, loose shoes and a warm place for bodily functions.")

What is striking about the Butz joke, apart from its ugliness, is its dismal lack of art: It contains no paralogical twist, makes no unexpected conceptual links; it is merely a clumsy enumeration of racist stereotypes. (Indeed, it is recognizable as an intended joke only by dint of its formal observance of the Rule of Three.) A comparable sort of artlessness is exhibited by the Auschwitz jokes that have circulated in postwar Germany. In these jokes the punch lines obsessively and monotonously turn on the idea of Jews being reduced to

Earl Butz (1909–2008). *American secretary of agriculture under President Nixon, he resigned in disgrace in 1976 over a racist joke about blacks. Earlier, at the 1974 World Food Conference in Rome, Butz made fun of the pope's opposition to birth control by saying, in a mock Italian accent, "He no playa da game, he no maka da rules."*

cinders in ovens. A catalog of Auschwitz jokes, with analysis, was published by the anthropologists Alan Dundes, Thomas Hauschild, and Uli Linke in *Western Folklore* (1983). A typical specimen, collected from an informant in Mainz in 1982: *Wie viele Juden passen in einen Volkswagen?* ("How many Jews can fit in a Volkswagen?") *506, sechs auf die Sitze und 500 in die Aschenbecher.* ("506, six in the seats and 500 in the ashtrays.") As the Jewish comedian Sarah Silverman has observed, "The Holocaust isn't *always* funny."

The superiority theory, augmented by Freud's theory that jokes provide an outlet for aggressive impulses, suits a crude racist jape like Butz's. Old-fashioned bawdy jokes jibe nicely with Freud, the repressed impulses gratified by the joke now being sexual. The Wildean *jeu d'esprit* seems pure incongruity. And the vast majority of jokes instantiate elements of all three theories in varying proportions. Hence the peculiar ethical problem with which jokes confront us: Telling jokes

that express a belligerent attitude of superiority—
jokes about the supposed animality of black men,
the supposed venality of Jews, the supposed slut-
tiness of women, or even the supposed humor-
lessness of lesbians (*How many lesbians does it take
to screw in a lightbulb? That's not funny!*)—strikes
us as unethical, especially when the butt of those
jokes is a vulnerable or oppressed part of society.
(Metajoke: *How does a joke made by a white person
about blacks always begin? With a glance over the
shoulder.*) Some of these jokes manage to slur two
out-groups at a stroke, such as this one, collected
in Belgium in 1970: *Why do the Americans have the
Negroes and the Belgians have the Flemish? Because
the Americans had first choice.*

Blasphemous jokes and certain kinds of lewd
jokes are also deplored on moral grounds by
many people who have perfectly good senses of
humor. Among the most religiously fraught jokes
are those dealing with the charge of deicide his-
torically brought against the Jews because of the

crucifixion. "Yeah, we killed Christ, the Jews killed him," said Lenny Bruce. "And if he comes back, we'll kill him again!" Or, in a later variant, attributed to the the Jewish intellectual Leon Wieseltier: "What's the big deal? We only killed him for a few days." Episcopalians might take umbrage at jokes that mock their church's ordination of gay prelates: *Why are Episcopalians so bad at chess? Because they can't tell a bishop from a queen.* Atheist jokes, oddly, tend to be more offensive to the devout than to their nominal target; for example, *Why should we feel sorry for the atheist? Because he has no one to talk to while getting a blow job.*

Then there are the jokes about women. The following, originally told to me with great enthusiasm by an Englishwoman, seems to strike most people as misogynist: *Why do women wear perfume and makeup? Because they're smelly and ugly.*

Some of the most repugnant jokes about women crop up in the vast volume of electronic chatter that takes place among idle traders every day on Wall Street. Perennial themes of the Wall Street joke (judging from the tens of thousands of specimens that traders have sent my way) are the desirability of golf and the undesirability of marriage. One of the more innocent examples (which also reflects the Street's quantitative ethos) is "office arithmetic":

Smart man + smart woman = romance.
Smart man + dumb woman = affair.
Dumb man + smart woman = marriage.
Dumb man + dumb woman = pregnancy.

More improper Wall Street jokes concern certain masculine prerogatives in sex. *What's the difference between a pussy and a bowling ball? Well, you could eat a bowling ball if you really had to.* Or: *Guy in a bar walks up to a woman he likes the looks of and says, "Hey babe, wanna screw?" She says, "Your place or mine?" He says, "If it's gonna be a hassle, forget it!"*

CAN JOKES be dangerous? Hitler thought so; "joke courts" were set up to punish those who made fun of his regime, and one Berlin cabaret comic was executed for naming his horse Adolf. The Puritans were notorious haters of jokes, a prejudice that can be traced all the way back to Saint Paul, who warned the Ephesians against fornication and jesting.

The idea that all jocularity was harmful to moral character was widespread at the beginning of the Victorian era. By long tradition, laughter was associated with blasphemy, with scorn for the outcast and infirm, and, above all, with obscenity. As folklorists have documented, the vast majority of jokes in oral circulation have always been about sex. Such "dirty jokes" served to lure the innocent into sexual degradation, it was believed. Women, in particular, were supposed to be too good to laugh. Only slightly less corrupting was

the sort of pitiless laughter directed at the misfortunes and vices of others, at the drunkard, the
cripple, the cuckold, the foreigner. It was the duty
of the decent, charitable man to refrain from jests
directed at such butts. This sentiment, by the way,
was not confined to English prigs. Baudelaire,
in his *De l'essence du rire*, denounced laughter as
springing from "the idea of one's superiority—a
satanic idea, if ever there was one!"

Around the middle of the nineteenth century,
however, a shift in attitude can be detected. The
joke impulse—once seen as actuated by feelings
of superiority, aggression, and lust—was beginning to acquire something of an intellectual aura.
Comic theorists like Coleridge, Leigh Hunt,
and Sidney Smith, taking a leaf from Kant and
Schopenhauer, put witty paradox at the heart
of jocularity. The word "wit" itself underwent a
semantic shift: Originally referring to intellect
in general, it came to mean an ability to perceive
connections between ideas, and then a quickness

at seeing the kind of incongruous resemblances that evoke delighted surprise. Joke-making ceased to be thought of as entirely disreputable, and susceptibility to jokes, at least those of the drier, more cerebral sort, became a social plus. Leslie Stephen, writing in the *Cornhill Magazine* in 1876, remarked that "a fashion has sprung up of late years regarding the sense of humour as one of the cardinal virtues." A few decades later Max Beerbohm observed that a man would sooner confess to lacking a sense of beauty than to lacking a sense of humor.

PERHAPS THE reason it is so hard to pin down the essence of jokes is that it doesn't hold still. The joke is not an unchanging Platonic Idea, but a historical form that evolves over time. Born of lewdness and aggression, the jocular impulse aspires to the delicate perception of pure incongruity. (Except, perhaps, at the Friar's Club, where this recently overheard exchange is still the norm: Shtarker #1: "Loved you in *The Vagina Monologues*." Shtarker #2: "So'd your wife!")

Consider the evolution of the pun. The earliest puns (Jesus: "Thou art *Peter*, and upon this *rock* I will build my church") were evidently not meant to be jocose at all. Shakespearean puns, while chucklesome, are invariably bawdy, even when they not being made by clowns:

> *Hamlet*: "Lady, shall I lie in your lap?"
> *Ophelia*: "No, my lord."
> *Hamlet*: "I mean, my head upon your lap?"
> *Ophelia*: "Ay, my lord."
> *Hamlet*: "Do you think I meant country [*cunt*-try] matters?"

The puns in a Tom Stoppard play, by contrast, are playfully sonic and therefore distinctively modern (as when a character in *Travesties*, speaking of the contrast between Lenin's modest birthplace and his subsequent career, says, "who'd have thought big oaks from A CORNer room at number 14 Spiegelgasse?").

At what rarefied telos is this evolutionary process aiming? Why, the Jewish joke, of course—or, to be more precise, the Talmudic joke. The abiding themes of Jewish humor are not sex and superiority but logic and language. Take this rather lame specimen cited (and explicated at some length!) by Freud: *Two Jews met in the neighborhood of the bathhouse. "Have you taken a bath?" asked one of them. "What?" asked the other in return, "is there one missing?"*

A better example comes from the comic Myron Cohen: *A Jewish grandmother is watching her grandchild playing on the beach when a huge wave comes and takes him out to sea. She pleads, "Please, God, save my only grandson! Bring him back." And a big wave comes and washes the boy back onto the beach, good as new. She looks up to heaven and says, "He had a hat!"*

At a more abstract level, consider this specimen, which has been known to transfix professional philosophers:

"Why should 'eretz' be spelled with a gimmel?"

"A gimmel? It isn't."

"Why shouldn't 'eretz' be spelled with a gimmel?"

"Why *should* 'eretz' be spelled with a gimmel?"

"That's what I'm asking you—Why should 'eretz' be spelled with a gimmel?"

(*Eretz* is the Hebrew word for land. *Gimmel* is the third letter of the Hebrew alphabet. *Eretz* is not spelled with a gimmel.)

Jewish humor deploys crazy logic as a way of coping with the incomprehensible. It is very close to

another jocular genre of great rarefaction, the philosophical joke. The best philosophical jokes tend to be
evoked by the most persistent incomprehensibilities.
Take the question that Martin Heidegger deemed
the deepest and darkest in all of philosophy: Why
is there something rather than nothing? When I
put this question to the great Columbia philosopher
Arthur Danto a few years ago, he brusquely replied,
"Who *says* there's not nothing?" Another Columbia
philosopher (and noted kibbitzer of the sidewalks
of Upper Broadway), the late Sidney Morgenbesser,
had an even better response when a student asked
him the same question: "Even if there was nothing,
you still wouldn't be satisfied!"

LUDWIG WITTGENSTEIN once observed that "a
serious and good philosophical work could be
written that would consist entirely of jokes." This
remark is a peculiar one coming from a tortured

Ludwig Wittgenstein (1889–1951).
The greatest philosopher of the twentieth century,
he thought a serious philosophical book could be
written that would consist entirely of jokes.

ascetic whose own sense of humor was quite
feeble. (A typical Wittgenstein gag was drawing
an arrow to the "W.C.1" in a London address on
a letter he was going to mail and writing, "This
doesn't mean 'Lavatory.'") Bertrand Russell used
jocularity to superb effect in illustrating points of
logic. Take the logician's principle that a contra-
diction implies any proposition you please. Russell was once trying to explain this at a public
lecture when a heckler interrupted him:

> "So prove to me that if two plus two is five,
> then you're the pope," the heckler said.
> "Very well," Russell replied. "From 'two
> plus two equals five' it follows, subtracting
> three from each side, that two equals one.
> The pope and I are two, therefore we are
> one."

For purely intellectual purposes, the most
devastating joke is what might be called the

Bertrand Russell (1872–1970).
"Two plus two equals five,
therefore I am the pope."

"spontaneous counterexample." It begins with a ponderous generality, which, willy-nilly, furnishes the setup. Then comes the punch line, which slays that generality the way David slew Goliath. Here's a specimen from Ronald Knox (1888–1957), the great English priest, Bible translator, and wag. One day Knox was being bored by a notoriously pedantic Oxford don:

> "There is only one aspirated *s* in English,"
> declared the don, "in the word *sugar*."
> Knox: "Are you *sure*?"

Another great spontaneous counterexample arose in connection with James Burnham, the political theorist whose 1941 book, *The Managerial Revolution*, was the inspiration for George Orwell's *1984*. As an old man, Burnham haunted the offices of William Buckley's magazine *National Review*, where he was revered for his gnomic bits of wisdom, known as "Burnham's Laws." A newly hired editor, fresh out of Yale, was introduced to the great man, who pompously intoned one of his "laws," something about the supposed wisdom of mankind:

"Everyone Knows Everything."
Said the new guy: "I didn't know that!"

The greatest of all spontaneous counterexamples—and quite possible the best philosophical joke of all time—is famously due to Sidney Morgenbesser. A few decades ago the Oxford philosopher J. L. Austin was giving an address to a large audience of his fellow philosophers in New York. In the course of this address, which was about the philosophy of language, Austin raised the perennially interesting issue of the double negative.

"In some languages," Austin observed in his clipped Oxbridge diction, "a double negative yields an affirmative. In other languages, a double negative yields a more emphatic negative. Yet,

Sidney Morgenbesser (1921–2004). *This New York philosopher, revered for his discomfiting wit, was known as "the kibbitzer of Upper Broadway" and "the sidewalk Socrates."*

curiously enough, I know of no language, either natural or artificial, in which a double affirmative yields a negative."

Suddenly, from the back of the hall, in a round Brooklyn accent, came the comment, "Yeah, yeah."

I have heard people say that Morgenbesser's "Yeah, yeah" stands as the funniest spontaneous utterance in the history of the English language. This is a rash claim. The funniest spontaneous utterance in English, whenever and wherever it was made, probably went unrecorded, and is now lost in the ether. Even among recorded utterances, Morgenbesser's is doubtfully the funniest. If I had to award the laurel, it would go to Oscar Wilde, for a retort he made to a now-forgotten minor poet, Sir Lewis Morris. The time was the 1890s, just after the death of Alfred, Lord Tennyson, and Morris was complaining to Wilde that his claims to succeed Tennyson as poet laureate were being neglected:

"It's a complete conspiracy of silence against
me," Morris said, "a conspiracy of silence!
What ought I to do, Oscar?"
Wilde: "Join it."

⚜

ONE CAN imagine the wave of Homeric laughter that coursed through the conference hall in
response to Morgenbesser's "Yeah, yeah," just as
one can imagine the gelid silence that followed
Wilde's "Join it." For sheer physicality, the most
splendid image on record of what might be called
the "higher laughter" is Boswell's description of
Samuel Johnson as he delights in, of all things,
an absurd clause in a friend's will (about which,
unhappily, we know nothing else): "He then burst
into such a fit of laughter, that he appeared to be
almost in a convulsion; and, in order to support
himself, laid hold of one of the posts at the side of
the foot pavement, and sent forth peals so loud,

that in the silence of the night his voice seemed to resound from Temple-bar to Fleet-ditch."

What is it about certain kinds of intellectual pleasure that elicits such a violent and spasmodic reaction? Marvin Minsky, one of the fathers of artificial intelligence, answered this question along Darwinian lines. Humor evolved to help us detect errors in our reasoning, Minsky claimed. When our logic goes astray, physical laughter serves to interrupt the line of reasoning and call attention to the fallacy. Minksy's hypothesis echoes Nietzsche's canonization of laughter as a cure for aberrations of pure reason. But other scientists, like the English brain researcher John McCrone, argue that laughter occurs not when we spot an error or an incongruity, but when we see it resolved in some clever way. As the sought-for resolution snaps into place, we undergo an emotional shudder of pleased recognition that issues in laughter. (*Why is it so hard to find the composer of the "Surprise" Symphony? 'Cause he's Haydn!*) On this view, the amusement elicited by a clever joke is just the fun of creative discovery—which suggests, implausibly, that the greatest peals of laughter should be heard when a monumental enigma like Fermat's Last Theorem is resolved. And, perplexingly, recent research by the psychologist Peter Derks shows that what makes people laugh hardest is not the cleverness of the joke but the speed with which they get the punch line.

Take my wife ... please! It is salutary for the would-be theorist of humor to return to this most attic and laconic of all jokes—due to Henny Youngman, of course—when the waters begin to rise up around him. The trick of Youngman's gag could not be simpler: Our expectation at the ellipsis is derailed by a switch from the contextually obvious interpretation of *take* ("Consider my wife ...") to an alternative interpretation ("Take her off my hands!"). I bother to spell this out only to prove a point made by Max Eastman, namely:

> the correct explanation of a joke not only does not sound funny, but it does not sound like a correct explanation. It consists of imagining ourselves totally humorless and most anxiously and minutely concerned with the matter in question, and in realizing that under those queer and uninteresting circumstances a disagreeable feeling *would* arise exactly where in our mirthful receptivity we experience a comic emotion. That is not funny, and except to the pure love of understanding, it is not fun.

What *is* fun is the way the incongruity of the punch line marks a defeat for a necessary tyranny: the tyranny of bourgeois morality in some jokes, of reason itself in others. We can rejoice in this defeat because it is brief and inconsequential; our reflexive laughter, an evolutionary token of mock aggression, signals as much.

Amusement at the contrived absurdities of jokes is an intellectual pleasure, the pleasure of finding connections or contradictions where none were expected. Although it takes place in the most recently evolved part of the human brain— the higher cortices—it taps into more primitive circuitry that we share with our simian cousins. Brain damage can rob you of your sense of humor, just as surely as it can impair your ability to grasp metaphors and make creative connections. Brain-scanning research suggests that, while the left lobe of the brain processes what the joke means, it is the more emotional right lobe that "gets" it. In experiments, patients with lesions in this lobe can have a terrible time distinguishing humorous from neutral statements (one "humorous" example researchers used was a sign in a Tokyo hotel: GUESTS ARE INVITED TO TAKE ADVANTAGE OF THE CHAMBERMAID).

A more disturbing discovery about humor and the brain was made quite by accident. In 1998 a medical team at UCLA was searching for the cause of a teenage girl's epileptic seizures. The doctors tried applying an electronic probe to various spots on the left frontal lobe of the girl's brain. When the probe touched a tiny patch in the "supplementary motor area," they observed something that was quite unexpected: The girl laughed. The doctors turned the current up a bit and touched the spot again. The girl laughed some more, longer and harder.

Was this a mere physical reflex? Apparently not. The girl claimed to detect humor everywhere in the sterile lab. "You guys are so funny, standing there," she told the doctors. They stimulated the spot again while showing her a picture of a horse. She laughed and said, "The horse is funny!"

Inadvertently the UCLA researchers seemed to have confirmed a claim made by a certain "Dr. Schwanzleben" in his work *Humor After Death*, that laughter "can be induced by the application of electricity as well as by a so-called joke."*

But their finding is certainly inconvenient to philosophers of humor. If, given the application of a little current to a spot in the brain, absolutely everything becomes invested with risible incongruity— becomes, that is, a *joke*—then how can humor pretend to be an aesthetic category worthy of philosophical analysis? (Baudelaire observed that the same effect could be produced by hashish, but never mind.)

The *New York Times,* exhibiting unwonted facetiousness, called the UCLA finding "a bombshell that could wreck the humor industry." Might the discovery of the L-spot render the cracking of jokes obsolete? That is doubtful. Jokes will always be powerful weapons in the hands of artful

---

*The oddly named Dr. Schwanzleben, whose identity is otherwise obscure, turns up in a footnote in Robert Benchley's analysis of humor, "Why We Laugh—Or Do We?" Benchley's own view was that "all laughter is merely a compensatory reflex to take the place of sneezing."

politicians and polemicists. Take the crack that Ronald Reagan used in order to sidestep questions about abortion rights: "I notice that everyone in favor of abortion has already been born." Reagan's remark is incongruous at first blush because it is trivially true: *Everyone* has been born. To make sense of it—something the mind does reflexively—one must switch to the assumption that there are two kinds of people: the born and the unborn—which is exactly the way that opponents of abortion like to see the issue framed. "The jester manipulates this mental machinery to get the audience to entertain a proposition— the one that resolves the incongruity—against their will," observes the evolutionary psychologist Steven Pinker. The audience is more likely to accept the incongruity-resolving proposition because it feels like a conclusion they deduced for themselves.

Putting the "ugh" in "laughter." *Sarah
Silverman, early twenty-first century comedian
and past mistress of the scatological vein of humor.*

❦

JOKES ARE products of human ingenuity that, at their driest and most refined, fall within the domain of art. Yet many people—even people blessed with a rich sense of humor—loathe them. Perhaps that has to do with the source. Freud claimed that the most compulsive jokesmiths are neurotics, because they are most plagued with strong impulses from their unconscious. We have all been tortured by amateur comics who cannot repress the urge to regale us with their jokes. Some have even been tortured by being made to tell jokes. Evelyn Waugh, convinced that his son James had no sense of humor, forced the poor child to tell him a new joke every day as a kind of remedial therapy. "In desperation," Waugh's biographer Selina Hastings tells us, "James bought a book of a thousand and one American jokes, and stammered through each day's instalment at lunchtime, while his father sat stony-faced, refusing to laugh."

A well-deserved brickbat was lobbed by Richard Wilbur in his poem, "To a Comedian":

> You stand up for the interests of folk
> Who need a bedroom or a bathroom joke,
> Told with a drumfire of such words as *shit*,
> To free them from repressions for a bit.
> It pays, you find, to give them what they're
>   after.
> You are the clown who put the *ugh* in
>   Laughter.

I hope I have not done that.

BIBLIOGRAPHY

Cohen, Ted. *Jokes: Philosophical Thoughts on Joking Matters*. University of Chicago Press, 1999.

Gutwirth, Marcel. *Laughing Matter: An Essay on the Comic*. Cornell University Press, 1993.

Martin, Robert Bernard. *The Triumph of Wit: A Study of Victorian Comic Theory*. Oxford University Press, 1974.

Morreall, John. *Taking Laughter Seriously*. State University of New York Press, 1983.

Oring, Elliott. *The Jokes of Sigmund Freud: A Study in Human and Jewish Identity.* Jason Aronson, 1997.

Paulos, John Allen. *I Think, Therefore I Laugh.* Columbia University Press, 2000.

Provine, Robert R. *Laughter: A Scientific Investigation.* Viking, 2000.

CREDITS

frontispiece: Raphael, *School of Athens* (detail), Bridge-
man Art Library / Getty Images

p. 9: Antonio Canova, *Palamedes*, The Image Works

p. 10: Philip the Great of Macedon, The Art Archive /
Archaeological Museum Salonica / Gianni Dagli Orti

p. 12: Lekythos, The Art Archive / Archaeological
Museum Paermo / Gianni Dagli Orti

p. 23: cartoon of couple in bed, copyright ©1961 James
Thurber, Rosemary A. Thurber

p. 25: Beatrice, The Granger Collection

p. 26: Joe Miller, courtesy of Schmulowitz Collection of
Wit & Humor, San Francisco Public Library

p. 31: Gershon Legman, courtesy of Judith Legman

p. 38: Nat Schmulowitz, courtesy of Schmulowitz Collection of Wit & Humor, San Francisco Public Library

p. 42: Madame LaPuchin, courtesy of Schmulowitz Collection of Wit & Humor, San Francisco Public Library

p. 47: Alan Dundes, courtesy of Carolyn Dundes

p. 51: Queen Elizabeth I, The Granger Collection

p. 58: laughing man, The Image Works

p. 64: Sir Isaac Newton, copyright David Levine

p. 65 (top): Baruch Spinoza, copyright David Levine

p. 65 (bottom): Joseph V. Stalin, copyright David Levine

p. 69: Sigmund Freud, Hulton Archive / Getty Images

p. 82: New York cabdriver, Chris Collins / Corbis

p. 86: Statue of Liberty, Library of Congress, Prints and Photographs Division

p. 91: Gary Shandling, Vince Bucci / Getty Images

p. 94: Immanuel Kant, The Image Works

p. 97: Earl Butz, AP WirePhoto

p. 109: Ludwig Wittgenstein, Hulton Archive / Getty Images

p. 111: Bertrand Russell, John Pratt / Keystone Features / Getty Images

p. 114: Sidney Morgenbesser, courtesy of Joann Haimson

p. 124: Sarah Silverman, John Shearer /WireImage/ Getty Images

INDEX

by Benjamin Healy

Page numbers in *italics* refer to illustrations.

ABOUT THE AUTHOR

JIM HOLT, a native of Virginia, originally came to New York to study philosophy at Columbia University and to go to Studio 54. He subsequently declined into journalism, serving, at various times, as editor of the venerable political magazine the *New Leader*, American commentator for BBC Radio Wales, gossip columnist for *New York*, and, most important to him, New York columnist for *Literary Review* (London) under the editorship of the sainted and lamented Auberon Waugh. He is a contributing writer for the *New York Times Magazine* and a longtime contributor to *The New Yorker*. He lives in Greenwich Village, where he has latterly been preoccupied with the puzzle of existence.

Made in the USA
Lexington, KY
29 January 2013